Moderating Workshops

Mascha Nolte • Stefan Kühl

Moderating Workshops

A Very Brief Introduction

Mascha Nolte
Universität Bielefeld
Bielefeld, Germany

Stefan Kühl
Universität Bielefeld
Bielefeld, Germany

ISBN 978-3-032-02416-9   ISBN 978-3-032-02417-6   (eBook)
https://doi.org/10.1007/978-3-032-02417-6

Translation: Previously published with SN

Translation from the German language edition: "Workshops moderieren" by Mascha Nolte and Stefan Kühl, © Der/die Herausgeber bzw. der/die Autor(en), exklusiv lizenziert an Springer Fachmedien Wiesbaden GmbH, ein Teil von Springer Nature 2023. Published by Springer Fachmedien Wiesbaden. All Rights Reserved.

This Springer imprint is published by the registered company Springer Nature Switzerland AG
The registered company address is: Gewerbestrasse 11, 6330 Cham, Switzerland

If disposing of this product, please recycle the paper.

Preface

Organizations take advantage of various occasions to re-align their own structure. When they explore markets, they analyze the organization's environment and discuss its impact on their own structure. In strategy projects, they define their goals and develop a target system aligned with them. In reorganization projects, they review how communication channels, decision-making programs, and personnel composition should be modified. In organizational culture projects, they analyze their informal norms and look for levers to influence them. In mission statement projects, they develop a set of values to serve as orientation both internally and externally.

How to proceed with market explorations, strategy determinations, reorganizations, cultural analyses, or mission statement projects has been described in detail. What has remained largely open, however, is how these projects can be implemented in concrete interaction formats. It is clear that each project requires a sequence of exploratory discussions, workshops, large-scale conferences, and web conferences—but we believe that there is no satisfactory description of how this is done in concrete terms.

This book is one of several dealing with interaction formats in change processes. The focus of this book is on workshops—that is, a format consisting of about a dozen participants who over the course of one or two days attempt to achieve a goal that has been at least roughly outlined in advance. Although in this series of very brief introductions we separately describe interaction formats such as exploratory meetings, workshops, large-scale conferences, and web conferences, we are always interested in how they relate to other interaction formats. We take the dynamics in the individual interaction formats seriously because this is the only way to get a sense of how they can be used in a comprehensive interaction plan in change processes.

In this respect, this book represents a fundamental change in the understanding of workshops that has emerged in recent decades. It is becoming increasingly clear that workshops only make sense in the context of a comprehensive development process, which is why the "before" and the "after" are central to workshops. We radicalize this idea further by seeing workshops as only one possible interaction format in organizational change processes, one which does not necessarily have to stand at the center of an interaction plan in change processes. In quite a few cases, workshops merely serve to hold exploratory talks or to verify the results from exploratory discussions.

In this book, we deliberately work with an admittedly highly simplified comparison between a classic and a new view of interaction formats in organizations. The classic view grants comparatively little space for the preparation and follow-up of content and tends to focus on the fact that central aspects come to the surface through the dynamics of the workshop. The new view, however, designs workshops that center on pre- and post-processing through exploratory discussions, and the workshop is seen only as a possible crystallization point for the discussion of insights, views, and assessments elicited elsewhere. Most workshops will fall between these two extremes, but juxtaposing these two emerging paradigms will help highlight the advantages and disadvantages of very different approaches to workshops.

While practitioners have devoted considerable attention to the process of workshops, they have been conspicuously under-researched in academia. Our primary goal is to present a practical book that will provide managers, staff, and consultants with the knowledge necessary to prepare, conduct, and follow up on workshops. However, we want to selectively incorporate insights from scientific research on interactions in organizations, because it is precisely by taking a close look at face-to-face interactions that we can gain important insights into the dynamics of workshops.

This book was developed as part of the Metaplan Professional program, "Leading and Consulting in Discourse." We would like to thank the participants of the various cohorts who not only critically examined the approach presented here, but also reported back on their experiences from the field, as well as the various interaction researchers who have repeatedly critically reflected on and commented on Metaplan's practice over the past few decades.

Bielefeld, Germany

Mascha Nolte
Stefan Kühl

Competing Interests The authors have no competing interests to declare that are relevant to the content of this manuscript.

Blurb

Workshops are pre-designed, moderated working meetings in which participants devote themselves to a specific topic in a context removed from regular organizational interaction. In recent years, the facilitation and consulting industry has seen a paradigm shift in the way workshops are planned and conducted. The new paradigm sees workshops as elements in broader interaction plans, in which they are complemented by interaction occasions of equal importance to them, such as contract talks, exploratory interviews, and large conferences. Whenever workshops are meant to bring about organizational change, they are embedded in a broader change architecture. This book illustrates in a concise manner how to weave workshops into a comprehensive interaction plan and thus use them as an element of organizational change processes.

Contents

About the Authors

Stefan Kühl is a sociologist at Bielefeld University and an organizational consultant at Metaplan. His most recent publications are *Führung und Gefolgschaft. Management im Nationalsozialismus und in der Demokratie* (Suhrkamp 2025) and *Managementmoden nutzen. Eine sehr kurze Einführung* (Springer Fachmedien 2025).

Mascha Nolte is a sociologist at Bielefeld University. Her most recent publications are *Visualisierung und Interaktion. Interaktionssoziologische Perspektiven auf die Methode der visualisierten Diskussionsführung* (Springer VS 2022) and *Workshops. Zu einer besonderen Form der Interaktion in Organisationen* (Springer VS 2023).

To contact us:

Metaplan
Goethestraße 16
D-25451 Quickborn
Germany
Phone: +49 41 06 61 70
info@organizationaldialoguepress.com
www.metaplan.com

1

The Workshop: What Is It and What Do You Use It For?

Many consider the workshop format to be a promising way to deal with a wide variety of topics and problems, and it continues to enjoy great popularity in organizations. For example, workshops are used for campaign and product development, or they are part of more comprehensive reorganization or strategy processes. In some cases, they are understood as an instrument of human resources development in which members of the organization are taught theoretical knowledge or practical skills, which they are then expected to apply profitably in everyday organizational life. Workshops with focus groups take place at the boundaries of organizations, with the aim of trying to identify the requirements of their environment and adapt their products or services to them. In urban and regional planning initiatives, participatory workshops are designed to ensure citizen involvement, and at universities there are workshops on topics such as effective self-organization and stress management.

M. Nolte, S. Kühl, *Moderating Workshops*, https://doi.org/10.1007/978-3-032-02417-6_1

In view of the different contexts and topics of workshops, this leads us to inquire about the unifying element of these events. What the term "workshop" means obviously depends to a large extent on the given framework conditions, such as the organization conducting the workshop, the organizers, and the professional context. The term is used in an arbitrary way in everyday usage, with a broad range of events given the label "workshop". Depending on the context, workshops focus on conceptual work, knowledge transfer, competence development, or sharing about experiences.

This conceptual imprecision, which is widespread in everyday language, is also reflected in the now wide-ranging practitioner literature on workshops. Here we find descriptions that do not define the term workshop at all, or only in very vague ways, with recipe-like implementation instructions that fail to draw sufficient distinctions between different types of events. This can quickly give the impression that "seminars" and "workshops" are synonymous terms for the same format.

The popularity of the "workshop" label format can probably be traced back to the positive connotations associated with it. In the English meaning of the term, a "workshop" is originally a craftsman's workshop, evoking associations of craftsman-like practice, collaboratively coordinated processes, and goal-oriented work on a concrete, presentable result. While terms such as "seminar," "training," or "education" have a slightly paternalistic connotation and sound like ways to mould organizational members who need development, "workshops" promise participation and co-determination among employees who take personal responsibility. In this respect, the term seems very compatible with a modern understanding of organization.

The term's relatively arbitrary, sometimes inflationary, and indeterminacy usage probably does not pose a problem in everyday organizational life or for most practitioners. On the contrary, if an event is called a workshop rather than a seminar, this may convince more employees to participate, which can have desirable effects on an organization's display side.

However, such a diffuse understanding of the term poses problems for a deeper examination of the format and a determination of what constitutes it. Therefore, we first need a narrower definition of the term. The following definition encapsulates our understanding of what a workshop is. There may be countless formats that aren't captured by what we understand a workshop to be, even though they operate under the same name; however, though they are characterized by completely different orientations, we should neither overlook them nor deny their usefulness.

1.1   What Is a Workshop?

We define workshops as preconceived, moderated working meetings in which participants devote themselves to a limited topic outside of regular organizational interaction. The topics discussed are considered to be too extensive to be dealt with in the course of everyday work, for example, in routine daily meetings or weekly team meetings. Accordingly, workshops have a longer time frame of about half a day to three days, and often take place outside the organization's own premises. As a rule, there is a concrete objective of what is to be achieved with the meeting. After the meeting, something should be different than before. The concerns are usually so complex that they cannot simply be decided upon by the hierarchy. On the contrary, it is assumed that the involvement of the employees affected by the issue—the various stakeholders—is required in order to make progress on the matter in question. Their views and interests should become visible and open to discussion in the workshop.

A workshop focuses on *conceptual work*: participants work together to develop ideas, measures and implementation proposals for the respective topic, which are then to be applied in everyday organizational life. Even if learning components or inspirational lectures can be woven into workshops, the focus stays on goal-oriented, practical work with concrete questions. Unlike seminars, the focus is not on imparting theoretical knowledge or, as in training courses, on learning and practicing new behaviors or skills. If there is no active integration of the participants, but only the announcement of prefabricated topics or decisions to an audience, these are presentations or lectures, but not workshops.

The complexity of the topics dealt with in workshops is also reflected in the discussions among the participants. In heated debates, it is easy to lose the thread of the discussion or to go round in circles. Avoiding such situations is the task of the *moderator,* who has established him- or herself in a fixed role in workshops. For the participants, moderators primarily have the function of providing relief; participants can concentrate entirely on the topics at hand, while someone else is responsible for keeping debates on track. However, the moderators' responsibilities begin well before the actual start date of the workshop. They are responsible for designing the content of the event and for clarifying the organizational framework. In the workshop itself, in addition to steering the discussion—for example, by asking questions about the content and constantly following up—they are also responsible for visualizing and documenting the discussion. After the workshop, they evaluate and process the results and conduct follow-up discussions.

Workshops are sometimes facilitated by the managers themselves. But often supervisors will be overwhelmed if they have to simultaneously take on the role of mediating facilitator and final decision-making hierarch in the same interaction. Because the demands between the two roles are so different, they are often difficult to reconcile in one person. For this reason, there are often attempts to fill the two roles with different staffers.

One option is to look for moderators within your own organization. Facilitators from within the organization are usually less expensive and easier to hire. In addition, if participants already know and trust the moderator, this facilitates preparation and can exert a relaxing influence on interaction in the workshop. As a rule, internal employees know the formal structures of the organization as well as the informal deviations and the interests of various actors and can therefore anticipate more quickly than external employees where the pain points of a discussion will be. As organizational members, however, they are also subject to the blind spots and taboos that exist in every organization.

External moderators have a greater degree of freedom than internal moderators. They have significantly less to lose and can therefore more readily afford to address critical issues. Particularly in the case of controversial, conflict-ridden topics, organizations therefore often resort to hiring external moderators. However, external moderators first have to build trust within the organization so that they are well versed in the organization and are able to lead sensitive discussions on critical issues. At the same time, external moderators are also limited in their scope of action due to their dependence on the person who has hired them and the prospect of follow-up contracts. External moderators can usually only address critical issues after prior consultation with the client. The external consultant's task is to identify these issues, discuss them with the client, and jointly find ways to open up a discussion about them.

During a workshop, participants form interaction systems that cannot grow arbitrarily. While there may be noble motives behind the desire to include as many people as possible in a workshop, the quality of the discussions will inevitably decline once a certain number of people is exceeded. This is because the larger the circle of participants, the higher the proportion of assumed passivity. A group of a dozen people seems to be ideal for ensuring that participants can actively participate. An upper limit of two dozen people is generally not exceeded.

Workshop participants are well-versed in the topic, yet are also affected by it. It may turn out that specific participants have to be present because they are the only ones who have relevant information, or are central to the subsequent decision-making process; for other participants, any person from a specific field of activity may suffice to represent that area's interests. The selection of participants is not a trivial task and does not necessarily derive directly from the topic; the client and the moderator have to think through this carefully together during the preparatory phase.

Although limiting the number of people participating in the workshop ensures that everyone can follow the discussions and contribute now and then, this still doesn't rule out opportunities for passive behavior. In order to involve the participants in the best possible way, to draw out their knowledge of the topics and to make it possible to discuss them in a larger group, workshops therefore often alternate between *small group and plenary phases*. While plenary phases initially serve to create a common initial understanding of the topic and to identify focal points for the small groups to work on, small groups think through specific aspects in detail and collect ideas. The facilitators are responsible for designing the small group work phases and for bringing them back to the plenary session in a meaningful way.

The facilitators are also responsible for creating a *dramaturgy*, which is a sequence of questions and statements that enable the workshop participants to think through their topic and develop results. Question and statement elements are interaction-triggering questions, provocative theses, or concise summaries introduced by the facilitators in the workshop. The chronological schedule consisting of the question and statement elements is composed in the run-up to the workshop on the basis of the preparatory contract and exploratory talks, as well as further research work. In the dramaturgy, the four ideal phases of a workshop—introduction, definition of the problem, consolidation, and conclusion—are pre-planned. The dramaturgy determines which moderation methods are used and when they are deployed, and at which time plenary and small group work is planned.

Facilitators usually think through the dramaturgy in detail and allocate specific amounts of time to the individual question and story elements. However, despite this fine-tuned elaboration, the dramaturgy always represents a rough guideline, rather than an irrefutable script, for the workshop. If the dynamics of the interaction develop differently than anticipated by the dramaturgy, the moderator must deviate from his or her well-conceived plan and spontaneously adjust to other key topics.

1.2   What Are Workshops Used For?

A workshop is not the right fit for every topic. The trick is to find the right format for working on a topic within the framework of the format. The scope should be neither too broad ("How do we improve our communication?") nor too narrow ("Which web provider do we use for our team meetings?"). Instead, there is a need for *topics of medium scope* that have sufficient breadth, but at the same time are sufficiently narrow to facilitate identification of the underlying problems and development of concrete proposals for solutions. The formulation of action-oriented how-questions helps to give form to a topic and make it workable.

How to Identify Medium-Range Topics

In projects for a large auditing company, the question was how to make the working environment more attractive for employees. The auditing firm faced the challenge of attracting and retaining good employees in an increasingly competitive labor market.

The term "New Work," which had been popular for a while, was chosen as the label for the employee recruitment and retention project. However, it became apparent in exploratory discussions that this term was far too general to define the relevant topics of the workshops.

It became increasingly clear that the central issue was whether there should be an entitlement for employees to work from home for one or two days. Previously, the accounting firm had made it the responsibility of the respective team leaders to negotiate with their team members how much time they could spend in home office. The result was a high degree of variability in the design of working time arrangements.

It became apparent that they needed a central regulation in order to enter the labor market as an auditing company with a uniform message. In the workshops, therefore, the main question was whether the partners were prepared to curtail the rights of individual partners in order to increase their attractiveness on the labor market.

It appeared that the appropriate medium-range issue was whether employees should have a minimum entitlement to a certain number of home office hours each week. This was clearly more specific than the "New Work" label, but not as specialized as the issue of the exact home office set-up, which repeatedly came up in the exploratory talks but was easily resolved elsewhere.

In addition to the scope of a topic, there are other criteria that can be useful when deciding whether to hold a workshop. Workshops are a suitable means when the issue in question requires understanding between different actors. They are useful when divergent views and interests need to be brought together. They are useful in opening up topics that are new to all those involved; a common basic understanding can be developed in the context of a workshop.

A large number of workshops conducted in organizations are aimed at one-off decisions that initially have no impact on the organizational structure. Workshops on event planning, product or campaign development, for example, serve to deal with routine organizational tasks, but they do not change organizational structures as such. Regularly, however, workshops also represent a means of working on organizational structures; in systems theory, we call this the "decision premises" of an organization. In these cases, workshops are an attempt to achieve structural changes in the organization through condensed, thematically concentrated communication among the participants. They are then usually part of change projects whose overarching themes—such as strategy development or reorganization—have a broad scope. In order to be able to deal with these larger initiatives in workshops, we typically hold a series of workshops in which limited, workable sub-topics are identified for each series.

Whether a workshop should be conducted face-to-face or online depends on various factors. Financial issues often play a role in the design of workshops. The difficulties of bringing people together in one place should not be underestimated in many organizations, and the ratio of travel time to workshop time is also an important criterion. What is crucial to the question of whether a workshop should take place face-to-face or online, however, is the tailoring of the topic. While some topics are better discussed face-to-face, there are occasions when the lower density of non-verbal communication in online workshops has its advantages. With complex topics that have a large spectrum of solutions, a high diversity of represented interests, and unpredictable actors, it is particularly important to also ensure the perception of non-verbal communication—such as the meaningful eye roll, throat clearing, or frowning. This is best done in analog workshops. However, when the solution space is smaller, the central actors already agree on many points, and their actions are predictable, the smaller bandwidth of online workshops, and the focus on the issue level that this allows, may be the better alternative.

2

The Opportunities and Limitations of the Classical Approach

Due to the continuing popularity of workshops in organizations, their design and implementation now represent a broad market for facilitators and consultants who compete with sophisticated methods for the favor of customers willing to pay. References to their own publications on moderation and workshop methods often serve to demonstrate their competence and promise to make it easier to market their own services. In the meantime, the practice-oriented literature on workshops is correspondingly extensive and often similar in the way it describes its approach. The focus here is mostly on the "event" of the workshop, with its internal momentum in the specific situation, while the phases upstream and downstream of the event seem to play a minor role.

In recent years, however, we have seen a kind of paradigm shift in the industry in which a changed understanding of the workshop interaction format and a correspondingly adapted practical procedure are becoming established. The conviction is gradually gaining ground that workshops should be

M. Nolte, S. Kühl, *Moderating Workshops*, https://doi.org/10.1007/978-3-032-02417-6_2

understood less as individual events and more as elements of more comprehensive interaction plans, in which the phases of preparation and follow-up must be at least as important as the event itself. However, this development sometimes takes place almost exclusively in moderating practice, and has so far made very limited inroads into practice-oriented literature. We start at this empty space by presenting—in a deliberately pointed and simplifying way—first the "classical approach", in order to subsequently delimit the "new paradigm" which is gradually asserting itself in practice.

2.1 The Classical Approach to Conducting Workshops

Most of the practitioner literature emphasizes the importance of comprehensive preparation for a workshop. Since thorough preparation is the essential prerequisite for the success of the event, it is considered important to lay the foundation for a successful workshop in this phase. However, "preparation" is usually understood to mean merely clarifying the organizational framework conditions—for example, coordinating the dates, selecting the participants and the venue, or sending out the invitations. The focus is thus on the *social dimension*, while the *factual dimension,* i.e., the work of the facilitators on the workshop topic in the run-up to the event, tends to be accorded subordinate importance.

> **On the Relationship Between the Factual, Social and Time Dimensions**
>
> From a systems theory perspective, there are three dimensions of meaning: the social dimension, the factual dimension and the time dimension. Every social system—regardless of whether it is an organization, group, family or move-

ment—forms expectations in these three dimensions. The *factual dimension* deals with the form in which topics related to the social systems are addressed. The *social dimension* defines which forms of social support are considered relevant for the formation of expectations. The *time dimension* determines how the disappointment of expectations is dealt with (cf. Luhmann 1995).

The requirements in the three dimensions of meaning often contradict each other. It is extremely unlikely that such behavioral expectations as "normatively strict" (time dimension), "factually far-reaching" (factual dimension) and "consensual" (social dimension) can come about in organizations, groups, families or movements. As a rule, the requirements contradict one other. If one wants to have agreement, one often has to do without a precise definition of expectations and mustn't be too aggressive in trying to enforce one's expectations in case of disappointment. If one wants to define expectations with great precision, then the probability of broadly support decreases.

For the analysis of workshops, the three dimensions of meaning can be used in a highly simplified form to make the contradictory requirements clear. If one wants to achieve a broad consensus (social dimension), one probably needs several days in the interaction setting (time dimension) and probably has to accept some abstractly formulated compromises (factual dimension). If the aim is to develop a precise specification of structural changes (factual dimension), resistance will have to be accepted (social dimension), and sources of power will have to be mobilized to enforce the new structures, even in the event of disappointment (time dimension).

As far as the preparation of workshops in terms of content is concerned, the practice-oriented literature pays little attention to this compared to the actual event. There is usually an emphasis on the necessity of precisely defining and examining the goal of the workshop in advance. In order to achieve this, clarifying discussions with the commissioning parties are recommended, while preliminary discussions with the participants of the workshop are usually not provided for in a systematic way. Where this is the case, the impression is often given that spontaneous, informal telephone calls between facilitators and participants are sufficient to obtain their views, interests and expectations regarding the workshop topic.

The reluctance to prepare content can be traced back to a view, still widespread in some cases, that too much planning could harm interaction in the workshop. In some cases, there are explicit calls in the literature to strictly limit the amount of preparation required for the event. In addition to efficiency considerations, the rationale for a procedure that spares preparation assumes that extensive preparation of the workshop in terms of topic and content leads to the formation of "blinders" that tend to hinder the moderation process and make it more difficult to recognize patterns in the discussion later on. According to this view, it would also be necessary to prevent the moderators, who are often understood as neutral, from exerting influence, as would likely occur during intensive preliminary discussions with the participants. The low consideration of the factual dimension in the planning phase of the workshop is inevitably reflected in the workshop schedule.

As far as the conception of the dramaturgy of the workshop is concerned, the practitioner literature often recommends open planning. Although the facilitators are supposed to prepare an introduction to the workshop, what happens after that must be kept open; after all, the focus in the workshop is on the participants and their areas of interest, and not on what the facilitators want to talk about. The latter must be correspondingly flexible and able to get involved in the dynamics of the interaction and to set the main topics on which the participants will focus during the event. The demands on the workshop interaction itself are correspondingly high.

The limited content preparation of the workshops inevitably shifts the focus to the event itself, which is then loaded with correspondingly high expectations. This event-focused approach is documented in the focus of practitioner literature. For example, there are numerous publications that deal exclusively with methods, tools, and games that can be used during a workshop. In contrast, there are none that focus on the pre- and post-workshop phases. The hope behind this procedure seems to be that the interaction will do the trick.

Thus, it is often still assumed that the meeting of certain people automatically leads to the points relevant to the topic in question being brought to the table and discussed. By creating a condensed interaction space in which the organization's internal expertise is gathered, it is assumed that a dynamic will inevitably develop that cannot be achieved in individual discussions or regular meetings and that will bring critical aspects to light. At best, this process needs to be supported by methodically skilled moderators who, through their targeted questions and rhetorical skills, manage to guide the discussion to the essential points.

Another central classical task of the moderators is the facilitation of understanding, as well as the establishment of consensus between the participants based on this understanding. According to this approach, consensus appears to be the ultimate goal of the workshop and the function of the moderators appears to be to navigate to this goal, at best by avoiding conflict. Accordingly, there is still a widespread view in some quarters that the central task of facilitation is conflict avoidance and resolution and that the goal of the workshop is to overcome "local rationality" through participation. This goes hand in hand with the expectation of bindingly committing oneself to subsequent steps on the basis of the understanding reached during the workshop.

According to the classical approach, workshops aim primarily to arrive at decisions. Alongside meetings, they are considered to be the places where decisions are made and legitimized in organizations. Whether binding decisions were produced at the end of the event has long been elevated to the central success criterion of the format, while the absence of decisions was interpreted as a failure of the entire event. This decision-focused attitude manifested itself in particular in the much-vaunted activity lists and action catalogs produced at the end of the event, which are often assumed to be one of the most important tools of facilitation. It was assumed that these lists, if they are just formulated concretely enough, could ensure the transfer of workshop results into everyday organizational life. Accordingly, their preparation usually marked not only the end of the workshop, but also the end of the moderators' involvement and the engagement of the commissioning parties with the topic; after all, there was now a plan from which all further steps emerge.

With regard to the follow-up of workshops, for a long time the emphasis was placed solely on the necessity of evaluating the event, for example with regard to the performance of the moderators and the satisfaction of the clients and participants. The need for an even more comprehensive follow-up of the *content* of the event was not recognized for a long time. Thus, the practitioner literature rarely provides for a detailed evaluation of the materials and results produced during the workshop, on the basis of which further rounds of coordination take place. In part, further work on the workshop topic after its end is still understood as an expression of its failure due to an overly strong focus on the workshop itself as an event and the widespread imperative to produce understanding and decisions *during* the event.

2.2　The Charm of the Classical Approach

The classical approach to conducting workshops has a number of advantages, starting with the spontaneous use of the format, which is made possible by the low organizational effort required in the run-up to the event. This makes the workshop a flexible instrument for acute organizational concerns. If we do away with intensive preparation, a workshop can be convened without further ado for any topic that arises in day-to-day business and requires the involvement of various parties. Whenever it becomes apparent that the standard interaction has reached its limits in dealing with certain problems, a more extended format can be used. In this way, the weekly meeting that is held anyway can quickly be extended to a half-day workshop and, it is hoped, the time gained can be used to comprehensively discuss all the points that are open. This approach also has its charm for moderators and consultants. After all, even short-term requests can be accepted if the preparation is limited to a few discussions with the client and a bit of research.

Facilitators and consultants also benefit from the low preparation and follow-up effort of workshops in the sales phase of their services. Since in most organizations the idea of the workshop as a single event prevails, intensive preparation and follow-up phases are often difficult to legitimize because the benefits are not immediately visible to the clients. The usefulness of preparatory discussions with a number of organizational members is often simply not recognized; after all, you have the upcoming workshop, where you will talk about everything. The willingness to make room in one's calendar for these services and to pay for them is therefore often low. If, on the other hand, the costs and time involved are limited to a single event and remain correspondingly manageable, the decision to hold a workshop at all is much easier.

The advantage of open planning is usually cited as ensuring a flexible procedure during the event itself. Accordingly, a detailed, timed schedule runs the risk that the moderators will stick to it even when the interaction dynamics would actually demand something else. Where there is no such plan, there is no risk of clinging to it, for example, out of fear of not being able to keep the spontaneously developing flow of topics on track. Instead, one can fully engage with the events in the workshop situation and decide spontaneously, depending on the topics set by the participants, which aspects should be explored in greater depth. Often, these representations resonate with a hope for the surprise effects of interactions: Through the encounter, something develops that one did not see coming and unexpectedly contributes to the solution of the problem. When every interaction has been finely planned and anticipated in the dramaturgy, the density of these surprise moments—which can of course also turn out to be less pleasant—will certainly decrease.

We should not underestimate the motivational function of the still widespread notion that decision-making should take place in the workshop itself. Since participation in the workshop mostly represents a membership obligation for organizational members, nothing more than physical presence can initially be expected of them. However, if there is the prospect of being able to influence decisions at the event, this can increase the participants' motivation to perform. After all, employees will only become involved if they are convinced that their efforts will actually have an effect. Therefore, even when it is clear that upcoming decisions will not be made in the workshop itself, there should be clarity about the fact that superiors will review the ideas developed in the workshop and how they will perceive them. If this does not happen, or if employees realize that their painstakingly developed suggestions will just end up filed away in a drawer, this will likely result in cynicism, indifference and a low level of commitment at the next workshop, especially if participants were promised influence over decision-making.

Working together on organizational issues whose relevance is recognized by all participants creates cohesion. This effect is likely to be particularly strong if, during this work, it is primarily the commonalities with regard to understanding problems and perspectives for the future that come to light. Dissent and confrontation, on the other hand, not only threaten interactive harmony, but can also have a negative impact on a team's or department's sense of belonging. A strongly agreement-oriented procedure that conceals rather than reveals conflicts therefore promises greater cohesion effects—at least in the short term—than a procedure that aims to reveal divergences and tensions that are sometimes difficult to endure.

2.3 The Limits of the Classical Approach

As shown, the preparation of workshops has often been limited to the organizational framework: the selection of participants, the search for suitable premises, and the provision of sufficient facilitation materials. Undoubtedly, these aspects represent a part of the planning that should not be neglected. However, where they take up the bulk of the preparatory effort, they cause a much more decisive aspect to fall by the wayside: the intensive examination of the workshop topic that takes place in advance, meaning a detailed consideration of the *factual dimension*.

If a comprehensive examination of the content of the workshop is neglected in the run-up to the event, there is a great danger of not getting to the core of the organization's pain and ultimately bypassing the essential issues. If one restricts oneself in this phase to discussions for clarifying the assignment with the commissioning parties and one's own research, there is in fact no chance of understanding the organization, the acute concern at hand, and the problems behind it. Without more extensive discussions with other stakeholders, it is not possible to find out whether the identified problem of the client concerns the actual pain points of the organization or whether it is more of an illusory concern that conceals other intentions. In particular, micro-political disputes and positions—which always have an influence on the possible scope for action—simply cannot be identified in this way.

The perspectives, interests and micro-political considerations of the participants strongly influence the interaction dynamics in the workshop. If they are not analyzed and related to each other in advance, there is a risk that unexpected thematic developments, lines of conflict, or camp formations will emerge during the event, which are difficult to respond to without preparation. This increases the pressure on the interaction and, above all, on those who hold the "reins of dominance": the moderators. They have to deal with this awkward situation and are faced with the challenge of both navigating the complex factual situation and acting as mediators between the conflicting parties.

The frequent failure to prepare the content of workshops can be traced back to an overestimation of interaction, which is still widespread in practitioner literature and organizational practice. According to this view, the meeting of certain people automatically leads to a productive exchange about essential topics in which conflicting interests become clear. This fails to recognize what most people should know only too well from everyday interactions: that interactions are—as a rule—systems striving for harmony, which always have only the choice to avoid conflicts or to be conflicts (Luhmann 1982: 84f.). In order to avoid the latter, interactions therefore tend to be mostly oriented—and especially where the "law of reunion" (Luhmann 1965: 170) prevails—to the establishment of a "working consensus" (Goffman 1959: 10) and thus to an almost instinctive pursuit of social harmony. One wants to spare everyone and oneself discomfort and therefore avoids the critical issues that would make this more difficult. The price for peaceful interaction is then staying on the surface of the topic, the controversial points of which are not discussed.

Between the Effects of Self-Censorship and the Momentum of Interaction

Every workshop faces the challenge that many topics are taboo in the organization. This is the case when supervisors participate in the workshop who would rather not know about all practices in a team, employees from other areas with whom there is a competitive-cooperative relationship, or external facilitators who, as non-members, are in principle first met with skepticism. "Publicity as a censorship mechanism" (Kieserling) is the term used to describe this effect in interaction research. In workshops with participants from several organizational units, from several hierarchical levels and with external parties, one cannot count on discretion. We would be underestimating the intelligence of the members if we were to assume that they would be willing to say where they see the problem under the conditions of an internal organizational public sphere.

The effect would be that members in the workshops would retreat into general formulations of values. Every organization has a set of values and formulas that can be professed under any circumstances (Luhmann 1995: 317f.). All members could be expected to appreciate these values as well. If one does not want to be completely silent in the workshops, then it is advisable to refer to the values cultivated in the organization.

This "public sphere as censorship mechanism" was observed in workshops with craft teams in a large French mobility company. The initial phase of the workshops was characterized in particular by a "strangeness" of the employees towards the internal organizational developers and consultants. In two workshops, it became clear that the team leader had previously told the employees that they had to act cautiously toward the externals. During the problem definition phase, topics were often chosen that were not the responsibility of the team. During the discussion, topics such as "vaccination against hepatitis," "disinfection facilities in the showers," "cleaning of the social spaces," or "information on annual working hours" were identified as being the responsibility of the branch managers, the head office staff units, or other service providers of the group, and were intended to distract from the relevant topics of the teams.

But the censorship mechanism in workshops can be overridden precisely by the momentum of face-to-face interaction. Exploratory talks provide information that can counter general value formulas. Pretentious rhetoric leads to fatigue, which can only rarely be countered by even more intelligently expressed value formulations, but does usually lead to a compulsion for openness.

This process was easy to observe in the consultation process at the mobility service provider. The information from the exploratory meeting, the duration of the workshops, and the repetition of topics meant that playing "bullshit bingo" quickly lost its appeal. Just by working on details of contracting, inventory management, or billing, more and more informal solutions from the craft teams began to surface, which could then be worked on in the workshops.

The circumvention of the critical points that is frequently observed in workshop interaction is usually reinforced when the facilitators see it as their task to create understanding, resolve conflicts, and ultimately bring about consensus. However, a strong focus on these goals often leads less to conflict resolution than to outright conflict avoidance, and thus not at all to the desired state. Where understanding is equated with consensus and the overriding goal from the outset is unanimity, tensions and lines of conflict that emerge in the interaction are quickly seen as pathological excesses that are perceived both as a threat to the interaction and as a danger to successful moderation performance. To avoid this impression, moderators—usually tactfully supported by the participants—then quickly work to bring disputants back toward each other and to create a pseudo-consensus in which people agree on points that are not in dispute anyway. Ultimately, the strong focus on understanding and consensus often prevents agreement from actually being reached.

As explained earlier, according to a still prevalent view, decisions must be made during the workshop and these must be documented in a way that fine-tunes subsequent steps and concrete implementation in the organization's everyday life. According to this approach, the preparation of action plans, lists of activities, or catalogs of measures is considered an indispensable necessity at the end of every workshop. However, experience has shown that complaints arise after a short period of time that the lists have not been put into practice or that they have been forgotten altogether. The general orientation towards a stringent, goal-oriented ideal model of the organization is expressed in the preparation of these lists and in the belief that they can actually be used to program organizational action. This results in a common "doer mentality" in management, which values immediate action orientation—and thus concrete instructions for action, such as action plans. But in organizational science, it has become widely accepted that organizational actions can only be planned to a limited extent and are much more often the result of favorable opportunities or constraints (see Cohen et al. 1972). If one takes these considerations seriously, it is not surprising that lists of activities often fail to serve their official purpose.

Even if we distance ourselves from the idea that these lists can actually ensure the transfer of what has been worked out into everyday business, there are still good reasons for such lists. However, these reasons often cannot be openly communicated. Only by signaling that one is talking about concrete actions does understanding take place in discussions. As long as there is no threat that what is being discussed could also have consequences, employees do not see the need to really engage with each other seriously. Only through the threat symbolized by action plans do discussions avoid becoming mere sham battles. Moreover, the immediate sense of satisfaction that participants feel at the end of a workshop when they see a detailed list of follow-up actions, which have been assigned to personnel and precisely defined in terms of time, should not be underestimated either. It is often helpful for the legitimization of the event vis-à-vis the rest of the organization to be able to present initial concrete results, for example in the form of lists.

Apart from the effect of the decisions of a workshop documented in action plans, we can ask how sensible it is to regard the making of decisions as the goal of the event. If there is an expectation that a decision will have to be made at the end, everyone will feel pressure to finally make a decision by the end of the event at the latest so that they do not come away empty-handed. As a rule, this pressure is yielded to, so that most workshops can present some form of result at the end. It is questionable, however, what kind of quality and sustainability decisions have that are primarily a product of the interaction dynamics pushing for the creation of results, rather than those made on the basis of actual understanding. In fact, there are numerous good reasons for postponing decisions rather than making them just for the sake of making them. For example, if important participants are not present, if further information is needed, or if a viable common path simply does not emerge even after lengthy discussions, postponing the decision may be the better, albeit initially unsatisfactory, path in the interaction. Instead of insisting on decisions, it often makes more sense to think through their respective consequences in advance, but to postpone them to the follow-up phase. In order to avoid raising false hopes from the outset and producing frustration in the end, the expectations of the participants with regard to the event should be managed accordingly.

The way to ensure that decisions don't have to be made frantically while still in the workshop is to provide a detailed follow-up phase, which, however, is often left out. Frequently, the follow-up—which often takes place immediately after the workshop—is limited to evaluating the event, suggesting that the workshop and the discussion of the topic are now complete. This kind of procedure misses the opportunity to actually transfer the good approaches that were developed during the workshop into everyday organizational life. In the vast majority of cases, these approaches will not become established on their own in day-to-day business. To achieve this, however, more is needed than detailed action plans for the future. If the follow-up phase is not deemed as important as the preparation and implementation of the event, the ideas developed in the workshop will quickly be shattered by the intransigence of organizational routine. What remains of the workshop is at best the pleasant feeling of having come together again and having talked about everything.

On the Ritual Order of Interactions and Its Challenge for Workshops

In a series of essays, the sociologist Erving Goffman impressively demonstrated the extent to which daily interaction is determined by tactful behavior and ritual practices. While society has otherwise almost entirely rid itself of its deities, according to a famous quote by Goffman, "the individual stubbornly remains as a deity of considerable importance" (Goffman 1967b: 96), one which must be protected and affirmed, especially in interaction.

This protection is not only directed at one's own self, but also at others. It includes tact, which Goffman understands to mean the support of the self-presentation of interaction partners (Goffman 1959: 13f.). Thus, it is a normal expectation in direct interpersonal interaction to spare the image of others, to overlook their slip-ups, and to do nothing that would cast a bad light on them.

Tactful behavior can contradict the actual views of the interaction partners, which they conceal in order to save face. Instead, a "working consensus" regularly develops in interactive interaction, which goes hand in hand with sympathy, mutual consideration, and the dampening of differences of opinion (Goffman 1959: 10). "A political accord is typically maintained, and participants who may be in real disagreement with one another give temporary lip service to views that bring them into agreement on matters of fact and principle" (Goffman 1967a: 35). The maintenance of such a working consensus ensures the continuation of the interaction and creates willingness to participate in follow-up interactions.

In sociable interaction among friends, in loving relationships, or at parties, the working consensus fulfills an important function. The willingness to participate in interactions would probably be low overall if the norm were unsparing honesty instead of tactful restraint. However, in interactions that do not adhere these model of sociability – for example, in workshops, in staff meetings, or in exams – the goals of the interaction lie outside of the interaction itself. The aim is to uncover the "real" views of the interactants. A superficial consensus quickly becomes a nuisance.

Wherever open expression of opinion would break with the dictates of tactful cooperation, it is to be expected that workshop participants will regularly keep a low profile rather than risk the disavowal of their colleagues. However, revealing divergent views and discussing them is essential for the success of the event. In the design of workshops, it is therefore essential to use "audience segregation" to avoid statements that participants would tactfully refrain from making in the company of their colleagues (Goffman 1959: 49), for example in individual conversations, and to find ways of making them discussable in larger groups.

3

How Can We Integrate a Workshop into an Interaction Plan?

In the facilitation and consulting practices of recent years, a "new paradigm" is gradually replacing the classical approach to conducting workshops. This paradigm sees the upstream and downstream phases of workshops as elementary components of interaction plans in change processes. The key to comprehensive pre- and post-processing is that much of what is supposed to be accomplished in the workshop itself according to the classical procedure can be achieved in the upstream and downstream phases. In the final analysis, the workshop is merely one stage in a multitude of discussions with one or more people in an organization.

But how do you integrate the workshop into a comprehensive interaction plan, and how do you conduct it in a way that connects as well as possible with upstream and downstream interaction formats?

M. Nolte, S. Kühl, *Moderating Workshops*,
https://doi.org/10.1007/978-3-032-02417-6_3

3.1 Understanding the Concern: The Contract Talks

When we start designing a workshop, there is always a concern: A topic that arises in the everyday life of the organization is to be dealt with in the context of a workshop. Regardless of who is the originator of the concern, whether they conduct the workshop themselves or commission others to take over the moderation, the first step in workshop design is to understand this concern. It will not be possible to describe the concern precisely right away. Clients often do not know themselves exactly what they are interested in. It is usually only in the course of the process that the thrusts of the various interactions become clear. But despite all the contingency in the process, an initial understanding of possible directions is needed at the beginning in order to get started.

In approaching the workshop, a series of questions have proven to be a heuristic tool in the clarification of the assignment: What is the context of the workshop? What is the reason for the workshop? Who exactly are the clients? What is to be achieved with the workshop? What needs to be discussed in depth? Who is needed to advance the topic? What interests do these stakeholders have? How long can the workshop last? Who will moderate the workshop? Depending on your knowledge of the organization, your level of involvement in the topic, or the preliminary discussions that have already taken place, you will be able to answer some of these questions at the beginning of the conception phase, develop initial ideas for others, and leave others unanswered for the time being. The answers that can already be formulated at this stage, along with the questions that still remain unanswered, form the basis for subsequent discussions in which it is necessary to explore the issue further in dialog with the members of the organization concerned.

If internal or external moderators are commissioned to conduct the workshop, the *contract meeting* usually marks the beginning. This is a discussion between the client and the contracted facilitators. On the one hand, it serves to elucidate the client's point of view: What does the client hope for? What is behind the assignment? How far does the willingness to act go? On the other hand, it serves to position the moderators: What are their intentions? What would be a possible procedure? What expectations can be met? In addition to these questions, it is also important to identify the key players for the issue in question and the participants in the workshop.

When conducting the contract meeting, one should keep in mind that clients are often ambivalent about their ideas; they often want something new to emerge, but are afraid of it at the same time. It is not uncommon for them to change their views in the course of the contract. For this reason, a single conversation rarely suffices to answer the aforementioned questions conclusively. Rather, it is advisable to schedule several contract meetings during the preparatory phase and to determine and narrow down the concrete concerns more and more precisely in these meetings.

3.2   Clarifying the Situation in Detail: Exploratory Talks

The preparation of workshops takes place in dialogue with the commissioners and participants, not in isolated cogitation by the facilitators. At least one-third of the workshop participants should have been involved in exploratory talks lasting one hour in order to get an impression of their positions. In the case of workshops on sensitive topics, it may be useful to hold individual discussions with all participants beforehand in order to understand the micro-political situation and anticipate conflicts.

An important function of the preparatory talks is to get the participants thinking before the workshop, to broaden their understanding of the problem, and to encourage them to become clear about their own position on the matter in advance. As a result, ideas are often developed or decisions are made in the workshop itself that have already emerged in advance and are correspondingly mature.

In preparatory talks, the participants' perspectives and interests can be explored and in this way it can be determined in advance how much room for maneuver there actually is and which proposals are worth discussing during the event. By exploring the distribution of interests in the preparatory conversations, it is possible to anticipate the dynamics in the workshop to some extent in advance and to set up the interactions accordingly.

The insights that the moderators gather in the preparatory phase can be prepared for the workshop and presented to the participants there in condensed form. This saves time in the workshop that would otherwise be needed to first create a common initial understanding. The time saved can be used to lead the discussion very quickly to the critical points.

Exploratory interviews are moderated, dramaturgically pre-planned conversations of approximately 45 to 60 minutes with one or more people from affected areas of the organization. The goal of the conversations is to understand the views and interests of those affected: What is their role in the organization? How are they networked? What interests are they likely to pursue? What are their views on the client's project? What problems do they see? What ideas do they have? Even before the interview, you should develop initial hypotheses on these questions. The starting point is always the organization and the position of the interlocutors within it. With a view to their respective positions, the "local rationalities" that inevitably develop through the division of labor can be anticipated to some extent in advance. The hypotheses obtained in this way can then be tested in the course of the conversations.

This enables an increasingly precise picture of the concern to emerge in advance, particularly through the comparison between different exploratory talks and the developing differences in perspectives. The contextual knowledge that increases with each exploratory meeting should always be taken into account in the subsequent meetings and the dramaturgy adjusted accordingly. In order to check and refine the ideas for action developed in the individual conversations, it can be helpful to introduce them in an anonymous way in subsequent conversations and to discuss them with other members of the organization. In this way, it is already possible to obtain a fairly accurate picture of what scope for action actually exists, where resistance can be expected for which proposals, and which topics are taboo.

In addition to preparing the content of the topic, creating expertise, and anticipating the workshop dynamics, another function of the exploratory talks is to introduce the moderators and establish a working alliance with the participants. This is particularly important when dealing with external facilitators whom the participants do not yet know. But even if the workshop is facilitated by internal employees, this phase is important in order to get in the mood for working together. The preliminary discussions create a common understanding of the problem. They ensure that the perspectives are also heard and included by the stakeholders who tend to hold back in the workshop itself. If a more well-founded awareness of the problem is already created among the participants in the preliminary discussions, and at the same time their own possibilities for exerting influence are highlighted, the acceptance of the event usually increases.

The contents and emphases of a large number of exploratory talks are easily forgotten. In retrospect, it is also often difficult to assign the arguments heard to specific individuals; the collected findings merge into an undifferentiated whole whose contours and contradictions are quickly lost sight of. To avoid this effect, thorough documentation of all conversations is an indispensable necessity. Since it is well known that the devil is in the details, one should not limit oneself to the occasional note-taking of key points or the recording of central findings after the talks. For this reason, visualization is used in the preliminary discussions, not only in the workshop itself. All preparatory discussions will be recorded simultaneously in both digital and analog form and will be visible to all participants. After the discussion, the visuals can be sent to the respective discussion partners with a request to review any necessary corrections or additions.

In addition to the documentation of the conversations, which forms the basis for their subsequent evaluation and the creation of a dramaturgy, visualization thus serves as a means of understanding in the conversation. Because the interlocutors see their statements visualized, they can immediately check whether they feel they have been understood correctly and react if this is not the case. Sometimes it can be meaningful to refer the interlocutors again and again to what has been written down, and to ask them to supplement and correct it. Sometimes the interlocutors get into such a groove that it makes sense not to interrupt the flow of speech; instead, it suffices to merely interrupt the conversation at key points to read out what you have written down and to ask whether it is correct and complete.

Since parallel co-visualization, which is visible to all, can initially be disconcerting for interlocutors who have no previous experience with it, the purpose of the visualization should be briefly explained at the outset. In order to ensure the necessary confidentiality, the transcript should serve exclusively to prepare the workshop, should remain in the hands of the moderators, and statements from the preparatory work should be introduced in the workshop in a discreet way that obscures their origin.

3.3 Writing the Script: The Creation of a Workshop Dramaturgy

The contract and exploratory talks serve to prepare the dramaturgy, the plan for the workshop. In order to ensure that the key findings of the exploratory talks are identified and incorporated into the workshop design, the transcripts should be systematically evaluated. The evaluation should not begin only after all of the interviews are over; it should start already after the first interview and take place parallel to the collection of further material. Based on the immediate impressions and the resulting visualizations, initial hypotheses should be generated after each interview, which should be referred to again in this phase. These can then be confirmed, modified or rejected in the follow-up interviews and through cross-comparisons in the material. Through an iterative evaluation process, one thus arrives at an increasingly detailed, in-depth understanding of the issue. In particular, the focus should now be on questions about the interests of the actors, the objective of the workshop, and the in-depth topics, which usually cannot be answered before the interviews.

Particularly interesting, important or irritating statements in the exploratory interviews are marked as "findings" in the material during the evaluation. It can be helpful to intersperse particularly concise statements, provocative exaggerations, or precise descriptions of problems in a targeted manner in the workshop. This ties the workshop discourse back to the participants' descriptions expressed in the exploratory interviews. Contradictory statements and divergent views are particularly revealing in the evaluation process, because they can provide important clues for the questions to be explored in greater depth in the workshop.

The results of the contract meeting and the evaluation of the exploratory talks form the basis for the design of the dramaturgy, which is a preconceived sequence of statements and questions that serves to structure communication in the workshop. In it, the four ideal phases of a workshop—introduction, problem definition, consolidation and degree—are pre-planned along with a combination of different interaction techniques. It represents a kind of script for the discussions.

Ideally, there are two types of dramaturgies. In a closed dramaturgy, all the statement and question elements are formulated before the start date of the event, thus providing a precise text and script of the discussion. The time for the discussion can thus be precisely calculated in advance. A closed dramaturgy is suitable if, for example, you want a high degree of standardization when the same workshop concept is carried out several times by different moderators. In an open dramaturgy, only the opening sequence, the sequence of problem elicitation, and some input posters are formulated in advance and the instruments for them are determined. For the further history one keeps rules ready to develop the dramaturgy at the process. An open dramaturgy is particularly suitable for the exploration of problem areas. Depending on the goal to be achieved with the workshop concept in the change process, one can choose rather a closed or rather an open workshop concept. In most cases, it will be a mixed form.

The procedure for creating a dramaturgy is the same as for writing an article: You start with the main part. In the workshop context, the main part consists of identifying and pursuing a deeper understanding of the problem. These are the phases in which the participants develop ideas about the topics that are identified in advance or during the workshop. The deeper exploration of the topic precedes the preparation of the workshop conclusion. Only at the very end is the introduction of the event prepared, with an introduction to the topic and the creation of a title poster from which the time schedule and the prepared topic blocks should emerge.

The dramaturgy work for a workshop consists to a considerable extent of developing stimulating theses, interaction-triggering questions, and inputs from the results from the preliminary discussions and small group phases. The precise elaboration of the interaction elements determines what will be addressed in the workshop. Once the individual interaction elements have been developed, it is important to link them not only in terms of content, but also to keep an eye on the interaction dynamics in the workshop. It makes sense to alternate between information inputs, theses, question elements and small group phases, especially with a view to the interaction dynamics.

In this development, it is worth paying attention to a high degree of precision in the preparation. Slight changes in the formulations of the interaction elements or work instructions can lead to other nuances in the discussion. Precisely formulated interaction elements provide guidance about what is to be done in the workshop, beyond the objective presented at the first day of the workshop. It reduces uncertainty about what exactly the interaction should be about, saves facilitators from having to refocus spontaneously, and allows participants to get to work right away.

After the various interaction elements have been worked out, they must be prepared visually. This can be done using flipcharts, posters, or computers. The timeline of the event and the rules of the discussion are shown on an introductory slide or poster. We recommend that this be kept in the room for all to see for the entire duration of the workshop. To create a good starting point for discussion, visually summarize the findings from the contract and exploratory discussions, which are presented during the problem-solving phase. By focusing on the key points and providing a balanced presentation of the different views, which are reproduced for reference on the input posters, tough initial discussions can be avoided in the workshop and a common initial understanding can be quickly established among all participants. Further informational visuals can be prepared for knowledge input if this servees the workshop's purpose.

3.4 Leading Through the Event: The Four Phases of a Workshop

The workshop can begin as soon as the dramaturgy has been determined. According to the format represented here, each workshop is composed of four ideal phases: Introduction, problem definition, consolidation and degree. We recommend a total of at least half a working day, i.e. about three and a half hours, for this. If a larger time budget is available, the phases can be repeated. In the case of a two-day workshop, for example, we advise conducting a closing phase at the end of the first day and preparing an interim summary. You can then point out the main topics for the second day or announce that the next steps are still open because they still have to be worked out "overnight" after coordination with the client. Instead of jumping right back in on the next day and seamlessly continuing the work of the previous day, this second day should also start with an introduction in order to bring the participants back into the topic and to clarify the goals of the day.

The workshop begins even before the start time. The event starts as soon as the first participants arrive. Here it is important to take away the usual initial uncertainty at the beginning of a workshop. This is done by creating places for "legitimate standing around." Coffee and tea are offered before the workshop, not only as a gesture of courtesy, but also to provide an "activity" in advance. Instead of putting out pre-made name tags, participants can write their names themselves on adhesive strips. Participant lists are available on moderation walls, in which participants sign in visibly not only with their name, but also with their length of membership in the organization, their location within the organization, and current projects, thus offering others the opportunity to talk to them before the workshop.

As soon as all participants have taken their seats, the workshop starts in plenary session with the *introduction*. After a short personal introduction, the moderators present the prepared program and the schedule based on the title poster. The schedule on the title poster is less comprehensive than the dramaturgy and only covers the rough thematic blocks of the event. This means that small dramaturgical changes can still be made throughout the event without the presented schedule becoming invalid. The discussion rules for the workshop are explained in this phase so that moderators can refer to them during the workshop. You can use a thesis to introduce the workshop, and all participants should indicate their agreement or disagreement by placing a sticky dot on it, thereby enabling the moderators to quickly call out pro and contra arguments. The thesis is intended to establish a substantive reference to the workshop topic, but not to anticipate the discussion of the actual topic. Rather, the aim is to create an introduction that gets the participants talking, familiarizes them with the visualization methodology and the rules of the discussion, and at the same time creates attention and excitement for the workshop topic.

Following the introduction, we formulate a *problem statement.* To this end, the moderators present the findings from the exploratory discussions. The participants have the opportunity to answer prepared questions that trigger interaction to point out ambiguities, make additions to, or question individual statements. This phase is important because it not only creates the interactional link between exploratory talks and the workshop, but also the basis for a common understanding. The common initial understanding that this establishes can then be built upon in the subsequent plenary phases. By means of questions prepared in advance, the exact problem is then unpacked. The moderators collect the participants' answers on flipcharts, pinboards, or screens. Some of the thematically coherent clusters of topics that emerge are selected for processing in the in-depth phase.

The topics selected in this way are worked on in the *consolidation phase* by means of questions that orient the participants towards action. In most cases, the topics identified in the problem-solving phase can already be anticipated at the time the dramaturgy is created, based on the contract and exploratory discussions. If this is the case, some questions can be pre-formulated in advance and prepared on flipcharts, posters, or screens. If these fit the issues identified in the problem-solving phase, the facilitators can offer them to the participants to work on. If this is not the case, these questions must be developed together with the participants in the workshop. Depending on the time budget and the number of participants, they then deal with the questions either in plenary or, preferably, in small groups.

Depending on the number of participants, the size of the groups should be determined in advance of the workshop; at best, three to five people work on one topic. In order to ensure interest in the content of the topic and committed participation, the assignment to the topics is left to the participants themselves. They can assign themselves to the identified topics, for example, by writing their names on small moderation cards and pinning or sticking them in the appropriate place on the poster or flipchart with the topic clusters. If there is an unfavorable distribution among the groups, the moderators must readjust, for example, with reference to the relevance of topics previously ignored by the participants or a group size necessary for the ability to work. Sometimes it is useful to address individual participants directly and thus establish an approximate equal distribution across the groups.

Once the distribution of small groups has been determined, the groups gather in the room. In order to avoid disorientation and an excessively long start-up phase, the facilitators assign the groups to their workplaces and equip them with sufficient working material so they can visualize their discussions and results. If at all possible, the small groups should stay in the same room, because the mutual perception of each other's work progress affects the amount of work and the pace. At the same time, since the sense of hearing allows for less selective control than the sense of sight, ensure that there is sufficient physical distance between the groups so that nearby discussions are not too distracting.

The thematic work in the small groups takes place with specific work instructions. Clear work assignments and a predefined sequence of questions ensure that the participants get to work quickly and do not have to agree on how to proceed. A question sequence consists of two to three questions and plays an important role in subdividing and deepening the discussion in the small groups. It encourages participants to think in different directions while keeping the discussion close to the topic and goal of the conversation. Based on the topic and the guiding question at hand, different sequences of questions such as "What is behind this? How could it work?", "What are the shortcomings? What ideas help?", or "What speaks in favor of this? What speaks against it?" have proven successful. If the consolidation topics in the different question sequences of small group work can be anticipated in advance, the moderators can already formulate the work instructions and question sequences in the course of creating the dramaturgy and prepare them accordingly. If, on the other hand, topics are identified in the workshop that were not anticipated, the facilitators should nevertheless by no means leave the group to its own devices; instead, they should formulate precise work instructions before the start of the small group work phase, which are noted down on one or more flipcharts or posters that are given to the groups. To ensure that discussions in the small group phase are also purposeful and that no contributions are lost, the moderators can occasionally remind the groups to visualize their discussions as well.

Following the small group work, the results are brought back to the plenary. In this phase, the ideas developed in the small group phase go through the "purgatory" of assessment by all participants. For this purpose, all of the groups present their results in turn. The plenary discussion can vary in scope, depending on the time available. If there is not enough time for an extensive discussion, you can limit yourself to simple follow-up questions that are not visualized. In a comprehensive "lightning discussion," participants mark during the presentation where they have follow-up questions or objections. After the conclusion of the presentation, the follow-up questions or objections are discussed one by one and the questions or arguments of the plenary are added. The small group and the plenary then have the opportunity to respond and continue the discussion. In both approaches, the aim is to sharpen the results from the individual small groups in the plenum and to incorporate the findings in this way. It is again the task of the moderators to ensure that the small group results are presented in the necessary detail and exposed to doubts by asking questions and, if necessary, making statements of their own.

The return of the small group work to the plenary session is followed by the *securing of results*. The aim here is to record the key results of the presentations and follow-up discussions. There are various ways of doing this. One variant is to have the participants mark points of interest on the flip charts or posters with adhesive dots and thus highlight key statements, results, or suggestions for further discussion of the topic. In another variant, the "walkaround" in mini-groups, the result posters of the small groups, fixed on posters or flipcharts, are distributed in the room. Then two to three participants walk together from poster to poster or flipchart to flipchart and discuss which ideas and suggestions should be recorded. They write down their thoughts on cards, which are later discussed in plenary. In another variation, the shout-out question for additions, the participants remain seated in a semicircle while the facilitators note down and add further suggestions and ideas from the participants on shout-out after each presentation. If, following the presentations, a selection has to be made—for example, between different options for action or concept proposals—a weighting question can be used. If concrete action steps have already been identified, "caretakers"—responsible people—can be appointed for them.

After the conclusion of the consolidation phase and the incorporation of the results by the plenum, the workshop must be concluded together. The *closing phase* serves to prepare the participants for further work on the workshop topic, for example by highlighting key findings again or recalling agreed steps for action. The "flash" technique, for example, has proved to be a good way of doing this, allowing participants to formulate a brief, concluding statement if they wish. Since this phase is no longer about substantive work or the continuation of controversies, these statements are not commented on by the other participants. The moderators close the event with their closing words, thanking the participants for their cooperation and referring to further steps, such as sending multimedia minutes or follow-up appointments.

3.5   Ensure Implementation: The Preparation and Follow-up of the Workshop

To ensure that the results of the workshop are reflected in the day-to-day work of the organization, the thread of conversation that runs through the preparation and implementation phases of the workshop should continue after the event. The preparation of activity lists at the end of a workshop usually does not suffice for the effects to take the form of structural changes in the organization.

The basis for the subsequent discussions is the precise evaluation of the materials that emerged during the workshop. This evaluation ensures that further procedures are not limited to the results that emerged at the end of the event—usually under time pressure—but that the entire breadth and depth of the discussions are kept in mind and can be taken up in the discussions.

Often, a viable decision emerges only after some time has passed and the events in the workshop have been reflected upon again in smaller constellations. It often makes sense to remove the pressure to make decisions in the workshop situation, because decisions made under time constraints do not stand up. The follow-up discussions, especially with those responsible for formal matters, lead to decisions that result in more sustainable structural changes.

The Problems of Not Having an Evaluation and Follow-up Phase

If there is no evaluation and follow-up phase, there is a high risk that the results of the workshop—even if they satisfied all of the participants—will not have a lasting effect. We were able to see the consequences of a lack of follow-up, for example, in a project for a large automobile manufacturer that wanted to optimize its international fleet sales by better coordinating the various brands belonging to the group. For a more coordinated approach to dealers and major customers between the sub-brands, the corporate headquarters and the country organizations in particular had to coordinate better.

Representatives from headquarters and one of the Group's country organizations therefore met in a workshop to discuss how the market could be better served in the future. They were satisfied with the concept developed during the workshop. However, the client was not convinced of the necessity of a detailed evaluation and follow-up of the work-

> shop and thus missed the opportunity to draw important insights from the workshop for their own management work.
>
> True to the motto "let them do it," the head office assumed that the relevant country organization would implement its specifications in the future as a result of their activation in the workshop. However, soon after the workshop, routine crept in again and the results achieved were quickly forgotten.

Particularly in the case of complex projects, we often see a slowly growing flow of exploratory talks, mini-meetings, workshops, web conferences, large conferences, and follow-up talks, which then ebbs away towards the end of the project. At the culmination of the project, the individual interaction formats always serve both to evaluate and reflect on interactions that have taken place previously and to prepare the next interactions.

While it is possible to develop a rough sense at the start of a change process about when to resort to which interaction formats, detailed planning at the start makes little sense. It is only during the exploratory talks that a common understanding emerges about which workshop form makes sense, and it is only from the dynamics of the workshop that it becomes clear which individual discussions, mini-groups, and workshops should be followed up.

4

The Function of the Workshop in the Interaction Plan

In organizations, workshops are always related to interactions upstream and downstream of them. Workshops are therefore part of an interaction plan aimed at organizational change, not individual events in their own right. If workshops are supposed to have an impact beyond the specific event, this processual understanding must necessarily underlie the design of workshops. In particular, where workshops aim to influence fundamental organizational structures, they must be embedded in a more comprehensive change architecture.

Even the designation of exploratory talks as interaction formats for the preparation and follow-up of workshops is imprecise. Describing these talks as preparation and follow-up suggests that the discussions are only conducted to ensure the success of the workshop. Yet the one-on-one conversations have an intrinsic value beyond the workshop. In the setting of a personal exchange, the discussion partners can present their positions, examine their own considerations, and develop new ideas. The dovetailing of the

M. Nolte, S. Kühl, *Moderating Workshops*, https://doi.org/10.1007/978-3-032-02417-6_4

conversations makes it possible for the participants to refer to each other without having to sit together in the same room. This generates an image of the organization that consists of various self-descriptions that refer to each other, which in itself can serve as a basis for change processes.

However, the central importance of exploratory talks in change processes should not lead to the erroneous conclusion that the workshop can be dispensed with altogether because the decisive phase has taken place in advance and the event itself thus only appears to be a "ratification body" for prefabricated decisions. The event continues to fulfill important functions as an occasion and as a reference point for upstream and downstream interactions. It is easier to justify the preparatory discussions by referring to an upcoming workshop. For facilitators as well as participants, the event date also functions as a deadline by which they must have completed certain preparations and be able to present their point of view. Simply knowing that one must be able to present and defend one's position in the context of a specially framed exceptional event frees up resources and mobilizes effort that would be difficult to achieve if the meeting were not held. Finally, the workshop has a legitimizing function, in which the ideas of individuals already initiated in advance are discussed by everyone and subsequently accepted or rejected.

But beyond their function of legitimizing and structuring exploratory talks, workshops have central functions in the context of change processes because of their own interaction dynamics. Here, the previously elaborated local rationalities of the various groups of actors can confront one another, thus sharpening mutual perception. In the best case, this can lead to a minimum of trust, because one learns to understand the motives of others better and can relate them to one's own motives. In workshops, possibilities for understanding can develop that would not have come about without a well-prepared interaction in a workshop. And sometimes you need a workshop—often several workshops—to enable participants to begin to see their own power in change processes and to be able to assess that of others.

References

Cohen, Michael D., James G. March, and Johan P. Olson. "A Garbage Can Model of Organizational Choice," *Administrative Science Quarterly* 17 (1972): 1–25.

Goffman, Erving. *The Presentation of Self in Everyday Life*. Garden City: Doubleday Anchor Book, 1959.

Goffman, Erving. "On Face Work." In *Interaction Ritual. Essays in Face-to-Face Behaviour*, edited by Erving Goffman, 5–46. New York/London: Allen Lane Penguin, 1967a.

Goffman, Erving. "The Nature of Deference and Demeanor." In *Interaction Ritual. Essays in Face-to-Face Behaviour*, edited by Erving Goffmann, 47–96. New York/London: Allen Lane Penguin, 1967b.

Luhmann, Niklas. "Spontane Ordnungsbildung." In *Verwaltung*, edited by Fritz Morstein Marx, 163–183. Berlin: Duncker & Humblot, 1965.

Luhmann, Niklas. "Interaction, Organization, and Society." In *The Differentiation of Society*, edited by Niklas Luhmann, 69–89. New York: Columbia University Press, 1982.

Luhmann, Niklas. *Social Systems*. Stanford: Stanford University Press, 1995

© The Author(s), under exclusive license to Springer Nature Switzerland AG 2025
M. Nolte, S. Kühl, *Moderating Workshops*,
https://doi.org/10.1007/978-3-032-02417-6